Sora Searches For A Song

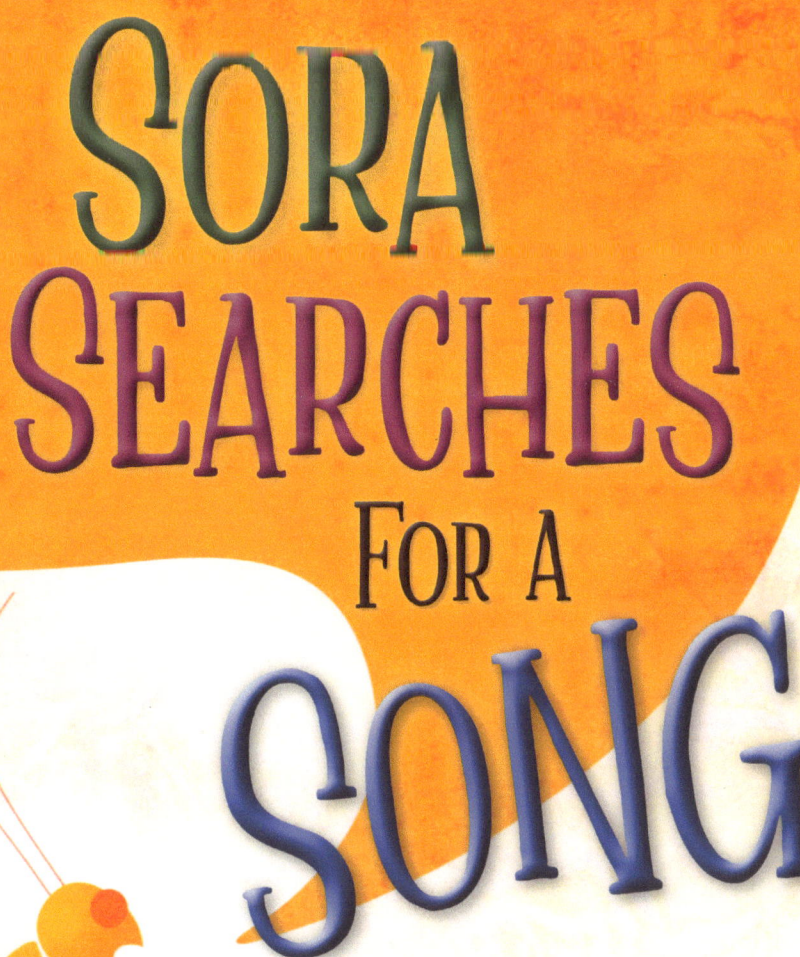

Dedicated to kids with big imaginations.

Once Upon a Dance

ILLUSTRATED BY SCOTT PARTRIDGE

SORA SEARCHES FOR A SONG: LITTLE CRICKET'S IMAGINATION JOURNEY
(A DANCE-IT-OUT CREATIVE MOVEMENT STORY)

© 2023 ONCE UPON A DANCE
Illustrated by Scott Partridge, www.jevaart.com
In Collaboration with Author Christine Herbert
Konora Photos in Collaboration with Dan Lao Photography
Royalties are donated to environmental charities through 2030.

All rights reserved. No part of this publication may be reproduced, distributed, or transmitted in any form or by any means without the prior written permission of the publisher, except for brief quotations for review/promotional purposes and other noncommercial uses permitted by copyright law. Teachers are welcome to use the story for class; please give ONCE UPON A DANCE credit.

Sora searches for inspiration and finds beauty and imagination. Will it be enough to awaken a song? Readers are invited to stretch, balance, jump, and move along with all the creatures in this delightful story of perseverance and celebrating your own unique voice.

Library of Congress Control Number: 2023903204

ISBN 978-1-955555-59-3 (paperback), 978-1-955555-58-6 (ebook), 978-1-955555-60-9 (hardcover)
Juvenile Fiction: Animals: Insects, Spiders, etc. (Fishes; Performing Arts: Dance; Imagination & Play)
First Edition

All readers agree to release and hold harmless ONCE UPON A DANCE and all related parties from any claims, causes of action, or liability arising from the contents.
Use this book at your own risk.

Other ONCE UPON A DANCE Titles:
Dance-It-Out! Creative Movement Stories

Eka and the Elephants	Dayana, Dax, and the Dancing Dragon
Brielle's Birthday Ball	Belluna's Big Adventure in the Sky
Joey Finds His Jump!	Mira Monkey's Magic Mirror Adventure
Princess Naomi Helps a Unicorn	Petunia Perks Up
The Grumpy Goat	Sadoni Squirrel: Superhero
The Cat with the Crooked Tail	Frankie's Wish
Freya, Fynn, and the Fantastic Flute	Danika's Dancing Day
Andi's Valentine Tree	Daryl and the Dancing Dolls

Ballet and Body Awareness for Young Dancers

Dancing Shapes   More Dancing Shapes   Dancing Shapes with Attitude
Nutcracker Dancing Shapes: Shapes and Stories from Konora's Twenty-Five Nutcracker Roles

Hello Fellow Dancer!

I'm Ballerina Konora. It's so lovely to meet you.

Dancing brings me so much joy, and I'm excited to share it with you.

Will you be my dance partner and act out the story with me and the creatures? I've included ideas for movements that could match the story. You can decide whether to follow these instructions, use the illustrations, or create your own moves. Get creative by trying different actions the next time you read Sora's tale.

Be safe, of course, and do what works for your body in your space. And feel free to settle in and enjoy the pictures the first time through.

Konora

ONCE UPON A DANCE, twilight fell in the great green marsh, as if giant arms of orange and yellow had pulled down the sky.

Frogs squatted on lily pads. Their croaks and splashes blended with the buzzing drone of dragonflies zigzagging above the water.

Crickets stretched their legs, arms, and wings. They chirped their evening songs, and the sounds all blended into a symphony.

Let's act out the story.

Imagine reaching up and pulling something massive from the sky with your powerful arms.

Now, let's move like the creatures:
- First, balance like a frog on tiny but strong legs tucked underneath you.
- Next, jump up! Flitter and dart like a dragonfly, flying quickly from place to place.
- Crickets chirp by rubbing their wings together. Reach your arms behind you, and rub your hands together as quickly as you can.
- For the cricket jump, start with your hands and feet touching the ground. Then, stand up and jump.

The cricket orchestra performed, but one little cricket, Sora, sat quietly. As the sound floated all around, Sora searched deep inside for a song. But nothing came. Melodies tickled across Sora's toes, legs, and back as the little cricket searched in vain for a song.

Then a stern voice pierced the night, and the music stopped. "Someone's not singing."

All eyes turned to the little cricket. "The problem is clear, Sora," the crickets all said. "You've got no imagination."

"Really?" Sora asked. "Are you sure?"

"Definitely," they replied as Sora slumped. "Everyone says so."

Poor Sora feels sad.

When I'm sad, I look at the floor. My shoulders slump forward and curve my back, making me small. Now, let's grow tall—I wouldn't want to leave you slumpy. Let's do that again! Repeat the curved and tall back one more time—it's a great warm-up exercise.

Try the same movement on your hands and knees. Curl your back into a C-shape, like an angry cat. Then make your back straight, long, and powerful. For an extra challenge, balance with feet on the floor, bent knees, and a curved back.

This was terrible news! Sora desperately wanted to sing. But how would it be possible to find a song without imagination?

Sora sat and listened, hoping to find inspiration in the nighttime noise. Cicadas hummed. Bats squeaked. Coyotes yipped.

But still, no song emerged. The little cricket settled into the grass, ready to give up and go to sleep.

. . . .

Close your eyes, and listen to the noises you hear around you. Can you hear your breathing, other people, a fan, or outside sounds?

Cicadas are one of the loudest insects. They make their sounds by vibrating parts of their bodies. Humming vibrates our throats. Hum by singing with your lips squished together.

Next, flap your arms way up in the air, like bat wings. Then stand on four legs like a coyote. Fill your lungs with air, and howl at the moon.

As the morning sun rose, the birds began to sing their chirps and pips and whoops and warbles.

"How lovely!" Sora listened for a bit, and then the little cricket's chin dropped. "I can't imagine singing songs like that."

"You can't imagine it?" asked the songbirds.

"No," said Sora. "I've got no imagination. Everyone says so."

"If you can't imagine singing like a songbird, become a songbird yourself, so you can figure out how it's done."

"But that's silly," Sora declared. "I can't become a bird. I don't even know how to flap my wings or balance on two feet."

Make a round sun shape with your arms. Sit silently for a moment, and pretend to watch the music float in the air. You could also dance as if you are the music.

Do a quick flap, and then hold onto a chair, couch, or someone's hand as you bend your knees, lift your heels, and squat down low. For an extra challenge, try it without holding on.

Try your "that's silly" look.

"Is that so?" the songbirds giggled. "Why, just take a look at yourself!"

Sora looked down and was surprised to see a finely feathered body the color of an orange sunset. Sora felt as light as air and took off with outstretched wings to ride on the breeze.

Make yourself taller, like a bird soaring into the air. This lift is a great way to get ready to do ballet moves. Lift even higher so your heels pop up off the floor and you have to balance on your tiptoes. In ballet class, we call balancing on our tiptoes *relevé*.

As an experiment, start your flap using different parts of your arms: your fingertips, your elbows, and then your shoulders. Which feels most birdlike to you?

Happy melodies poured out of Sora's tiny open beak and echoed through the clouds. They were as lovely as any songbird's.

Sora twittered and cheeped and chattered and peeped. What fine new sounds! Sora could whistle and trill and cluck and coo.

· ·

How many different sounds can you make with just your mouth?

Choose a favorite and circle your head around, sending music to all the corners of the room.

Long shadows and soft yellow reflected off a nearby pond in the morning sun.

Sora glided toward the water. Ripples danced as the little bird set down on the pond's surface.

Sora sipped the cool waters, gently dipped each wing for a bath, then dried off in the sunshine.

· ·

Let's tiptoe and imagine softly skimming the top of the water.

Bend forward to get your imaginary drink.

Reach each arm out to stretch as far sideways as you can go, as if you want to get your wing wet but keep the rest of you dry.

Soon, a school of little fish gathered below. Sora was impressed with how the fish swam so close without bumping into each other.

"That looks like fun!" said Sora. "I can't imagine living under the water like that."

"You can't imagine it? Are you sure?" the fish asked.

"I'm sure," said Sora with a sigh. "I've got no imagination. Everyone says so."

"In that case, you'll need to become a fish yourself to see how it's done," said the fish, swaying their bodies from side to side.

. . . .

Put your hands together in front of you, and let your fingertips lead you in soft, swirly sweeps right and left, like a fish. If you have a friend, take turns following each other but never touching.

Sora couldn't argue with that logic. Sora dove into the water and joined them. They swished and wiggled and splashed and jiggled.

Sora tried singing an underwater song. "Bub, bub, glub!" burbled up to the water's surface. It was followed by, "Gloop, gloop, bloop!"

The bubbles of music led away from the little fish, and Sora swam off to follow the song.

Soon, Sora was surrounded by much larger fish who looked . . . hungry.

Lift your arms above your head with your palms touching each other. Push your fingertips up, forward, then down to the ground. Let your body follow, and lie down.

Splish splash all your body parts.

Sora raced back to where the school of little fish had been playing, but only frogs, turtles, and slithery snakes remained. Sora dashed behind a tangle of tree roots at the water's edge, trying very hard to look *not delicious*.

"Come here, little one," called a hungry creature. "I wish to eat you."

"Surely there must be something better to eat than me," said Sora. "What about these tree roots?"

"Tree roots taste terrible," the creature said. "Trees are tough and bitter and chock full of splinters. I would get a bellyache if I crunched on trees."

"I can't imagine it's as bad as all that," said Sora. "How tough could a tree possibly be?"

Let's move like the animals. Do a few more frog jumps. If you want an extra challenge, pull your feet up while you're in the air. Scrunch your head into your turtle shell, then peek out. Lie down on your belly, scooch forward like a snake, then press up to look around.

Curl up small to hide like Sora.

As soon as the words *I can't imagine* came out, Sora realized what a mistake it was to speak them.

But it was too late!

Sora's body stretched, strained, prickled, and bristled as it turned to trunk and bark. Poor Sora had never felt so uncomfortable!

Let's turn all our muscles on and feel strong. Press your feet into the ground like roots, and stretch the top of your head toward the ceiling. Extend your arms like sturdy branches. If someone tried to move your arms or legs, they would stay stuck.

Try reaching your arms in different directions. Where do you feel the strongest?

Sora tried to move, but everything felt too heavy. Even after twisting, reaching, shrinking, jumping, and shouting, Sora's body hardly budged.

Sora wished more than anything to be a little cricket again.

If only I could stop this nightmare! thought Sora, eyes squeezing shut.

How can I make it stop?

I must open my eyes!

....

Imagine the wind whips around your trunk. Keep your feet reaching into the ground as you gently twist your shoulders. With your legs frozen, push your belly button backward and forward so your feet and head stay still but your belly moves a little.

Try to jump without leaving the ground, as if your roots keep you stuck, stuck, stuck.

Close your eyes tight and shake your head.

Sora blinked and found not a tree, nor a fish, nor a bird—just a little cricket with a big imagination!

Sounds gathered in Sora's belly, back, arms, and legs, and when they escaped, the melody surprised and delighted. The music reminded Sora of flight, frenzy, friendship, fear, and freedom. It was an original song—a big and marvelous song—bursting with imagination.

Everyone said so.

Thee End.
The End.

(My grandpa always ended stories this way, and I like to share the fun.)

I'd love to see your happy dance, like a little cricket soaring in happiness.

Thanks for being my dance partner. I hope you'll keep a song in your heart until our next adventure.

Love,

Konora

Did you enjoy our imagination deep dive?

Once Upon a Dance is a mother-daughter team. Both of us were happily immersed in the deep end of the ballet world until 2020 and the pandemic. We *just keep swimming* and making stories, even though it's difficult to get the word out. We donate our 25 books to libraries, teachers, and dance instructors, and donate all proceeds to charity partners, in an effort to get books in the hands of more kids.

Reviews encourage folks to take a chance on this self-published story, and we'd be immensely grateful for a kind, honest review from a grown-up on Amazon or Goodreads or a shout-out or follow on social media if you enjoy our Dance-It-Out! series. Thank you!

@Once_UponADance (Instagram)
OnceUponADanceViralDancing (Facebook)

CHECK OUT OUR OTHER BOOKS!

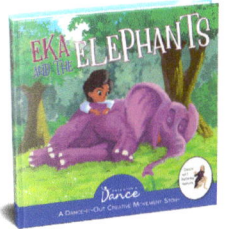 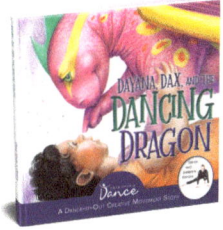  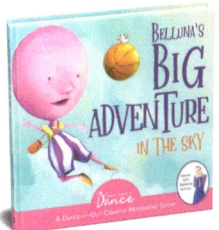 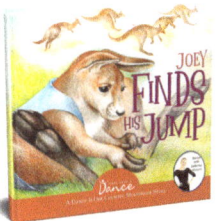

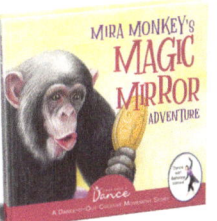 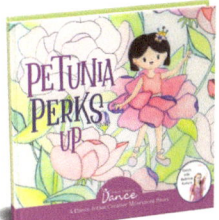 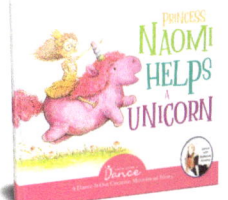  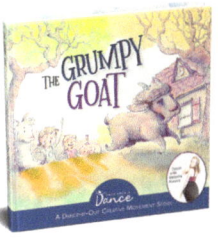 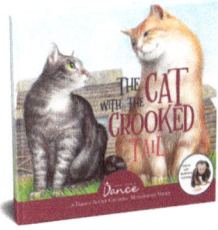

 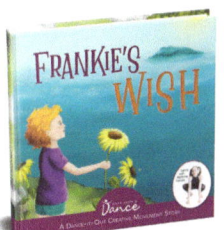 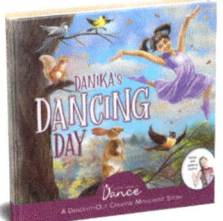 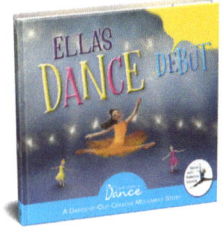 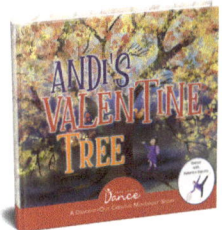 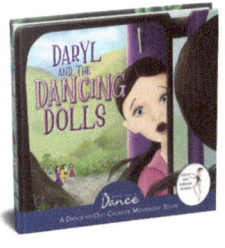

CPSIA information can be obtained
at www.ICGtesting.com
Printed in the USA
JSHW041813110623
42989JS00004B/123